Original title:
Life: A Mystery I'm Still Solving

Copyright © 2025 Creative Arts Management OÜ
All rights reserved.

Author: Adeline Fairfax
ISBN HARDBACK: 978-1-80566-195-5
ISBN PAPERBACK: 978-1-80566-490-1

Raindrops of Reflection

Frogs in hats are singing loud,
While umbrellas dance in the crowd.
Puddles hold stories, quite absurd,
Like ducks reciting every word.

Each drop a secret, each drip a clue,
Why do squirrels wear shoes that are blue?
With every splash, a riddle to face,
In this rain, we find our place.

The Pulse of the Unsung

A cat plays chess with a clever mouse,
While shadows whisper in the house.
Tick-tock, the clock has gone mad,
Stealing cookies, it's quite the fad.

Mice in tuxedos dance with flair,
While socks debate who has the best pair.
Laughter fills the corners of night,
As dreams take off in a silly flight.

Fragments of a Revealed Picture

A puzzle piece shaped like a shoe,
Sits next to a rainbow oddly askew.
Cups of coffee argue with tea,
About who brews the best cup, you see.

The cat's got the grumpy old bird,
Who mutters jokes that are truly absurd.
Can't find the edge, it's so unfair,
This jigsaw life can give you a scare.

The Echo of Hidden Truths

Whispers echo from behind closed doors,
Where imaginations create wild wars.
A spoon claims it's a shovel today,
As forks tell knives, 'Let's run away!'

Turtles gossip about speedy snails,
While a fish forecasts, 'Beware of gales!'
Hidden truths tickle our silly bones,
As laughter echoes through playful tones.

Navigating the Fog

In the mist, I take a step,
The ground feels like a giant pep.
A twist, a turn, oh what a flip,
Where's my coffee? Need a sip.

A squirrel steals my sandwich treat,
While I'm lost, searching my feet.
A map drawn by an old cat's paw,
This navigation needs a law.

Maps of Forgotten Dreams

I found a map, with a red X,
Turns out it's just a box of flex.
With crayons drawn in vibrant craze,
Adventures mapped in childhood days.

The treasure chest, a joke indeed,
Full of toys and old receipts.
Were we ever meant to find,
What's hidden in the playful mind?

Clues in the Dust

In the attic dust, my fortune lies,
Among old shoes and funky ties.
A clue scribbled on a sock,
Is that a treasure? Or just a rock?

I see the signs, they make no sense,
Was that a clue or just pretense?
The vacuum cleaner stole my trail,
Helpless, I howl like a wailing whale.

Starlight on the Path

Under the stars, I strut and sway,
Trip over dreams, simply on display.
A shooting star? No, just a cat,
With all my hopes, where's the welcome mat?

I dance with shadows, make them cheer,
They tell me jokes I barely hear.
Yet in this chaos, I still grin,
For every stumble's a chance to win.

Mosaic of Moments

Juggling thoughts like fruits in air,
Sometimes I drop one, but who'll care?
Each splash of joy, a clumsy dance,
Turns awkward steps into a chance.

Paths twist like spaghetti on a plate,
What's for dinner? I can't quite state!
Hearts flap like birds with silly wings,
Chasing the laughter that life brings.

The Colors of Uncertainty

Painting the walls with paint that's wet,
Oops! I stepped in and now I fret.
Each stroke of doubt, a splash of cheer,
Turns muddy mess into something dear.

Filling my cup with questions galore,
Pouring too much, it spills on the floor!
Yet puddles form, and there I stand,
Splashing joy with a clumsy hand.

Capturing Ephemeral Truths

I chase the cat who's taken my pen,
She writes her tales; I can't join them!
Each whisker twitch, a clue from fate,
But I still can't figure out this plate!

Snapshots fade like last night's dreams,
My camera's broken, or so it seems.
Nonetheless, I giggle, drop the chase,
"Capture" feels like a workplace race!

Veiled Horizons

Dancing past mirrors that don't reflect,
I wave high to strangers, what did I expect?
The fog is thick, like a soup on the boil,
   Stirring my thoughts, oh what a toil!

Peeking through curtains, don't know what's near,
Is that tomorrow, or just my fear?
Yet with each giggle, the clouds drift by,
   I'll ride this wave, oh me, oh my!

Secrets Behind Closed Doors

Behind the door, the cat has schemes,
Plotting joy in silent dreams.
With every creak, a secret's told,
As socks and snacks are called to bold.

A sock thief lurks; it's quite the tale,
With crumbs of cookies on the trail.
In every corner, laughter hides,
Our shenanigans, our hearts collide.

What's in that box? A shoe? A hat?
The dog looks pleased; he thinks it's that.
Dancing shadows, playful spooks,
What nonsense lives in those old nooks!

So here's the truth: we're best of friends,
In all the madness, joy transcends.
Peek through the door, if you dare to see,
The quirky riddle of you and me.

The Horizon of the Unexpected

A spoon just flew, my soup took flight,
Did a ghost dance in the pale moonlight?
The horizon's bright with chance's grin,
Oh, what a ride, let the fun begin!

A parrot learned to sing my tune,
While squirrels plotted by the dune.
Bubbles linger in the fruitcake fog,
What's lurking near the family dog?

The toaster jumped; it's quite absurd,
To find my breakfast flipping, stirred.
Under the sun, the world does prance,
In every moment, we find a chance.

Tomorrow's dawn leads to new delight,
No telling what will explode in sight.
So grab your hat and dance along,
To life's strange rhythm, beat the throng!

Patterns in the Mystery

I found some crumbs and a broken toy,
The cat's expression? Purest joy.
My shoes still missing, not a clue,
Was it the toddler? Or the zoo?

A puzzle piece is hiding there,
Behind the couch, with an old teddy bear.
The search uncovers truths quite strange,
Like how the dog thinks socks are change.

Each day unfolds like a comic strip,
With wild adventures on this trip.
What's coming next, a clown or a tree?
In this grand tale, who will be free?

Patterns swirl in a humorous dance,
With tangled yarn, it seems, by chance.
So let's embrace each riddle's flight,
And laugh together into the night.

The Tides of Inquiry

The waves crash loud, the questions flow,
What's in the tide? Ah, who would know?
With every splash, a chuckle's born,
As seashells giggle, the sand is worn.

Tidepools glow with mysteries bright,
Fish wear sunglasses, what a sight!
A crab walks sideways, dare to ask?
In ocean's court, it takes to task.

What's lurking there? A pirate's loot?
Or maybe just a runaway boot?
In every tide, a story's spun,
Full of delight, and never done.

So sail along, the sea is wide,
With whimsy, joy, and the playful tide.
Let every wave find humor true,
In this ocean of wonders, just me and you.

Unraveled Threads

In the loom of time, knots appear,
Each twist and turn, a strand sincere.
With laughter loud, I tug at fate,
What's tangled up? Oh, isn't it great!

A sock that vanished, a shoe on the roof,
I chase the clues, trying to find proof.
Who hid the remote? Was it the cat?
In this tangled web, I ponder that spat!

The cereal box claims it's a prize,
A maze to solve with a cupcake surprise.
I munch on confusion, sprinkle in cheer,
Life's riddle wrapped in morning's veneer.

But with every laugh, I find a thread,
Stitching my questions as I forge ahead.
With humor as my guide through this lore,
I unravel more, always craving for more.

The Puzzle Box of Existence

A box on the shelf, it rattles with glee,
Open me up, there's treasure, you see!
But inside is a sock and a half-eaten treat,
What a curious mystery, isn't that neat?

The pieces collide, like birds gone astray,
Flapping around with much to say.
I'm missing a corner, the picture's askew,
What's this strange puzzle? Oh, just a shoe!

Instructions are lacking, the rules are all bent,
My attempts at assembly? A life well spent.
With giggles I chase each wild little fact,
Each whimsical turn in this curious act.

As I pry open drawers, new games I retrieve,
Life chuckles along, "What do you believe?"
I'll keep spinning this box, oh what a thrill,
These odd little moments, I'm savoring still.

Sensations of the Unfamiliar

A tickle on my nose, is it dust or a bug?
The unknown welcomes me, with a warm little hug.
I tiptoe on feelings, with mismatched delight,
Exploring the edges of what's wrong and right.

The chair creaks softly, a haunted praise,
I laugh with shadows that dance in a haze.
Odd snacks on the table, a sight to behold,
Pickles and jelly, a story retold!

Through blunders and giggles, I wander with cheer,
What would I learn if I ventured up here?
A mix of sensations, both weird and profound,
Turns out it's fun, this odd little round!

With each wobbly step, I stumble and grin,
Embracing the strangeness, the chaos within.
In this joyful peculiar, I've found my own spark,
What's familiar is fun, like a walk in the dark.

Atlas of the Heart's Queries

My heart is a map, with roads that confound,
Each question a highway, twisting around.
Where to go next? The signs are a mess,
But joy in the journey? Oh, that's the best!

I plot my adventures with crayons and flair,
Drawing wild routes in the cool evening air.
With laughter as fuel, the compass spun right,
I wander these paths, oh what a delight!

The landmarks of friendship, memories formed,
With every new turn, new joys are transformed.
The laughs that we share, oh they draw me in close,
In the atlas of heartstrings, I'll forever engross.

So here's to the questions, the laughter, the fun,
In this puzzle of living, I'll never be done.
With each curious glance, I set forth with cheer,
Mapping my journey, for more laughs to appear.

The Chronicles of Curiosity

Why do socks vanish, it's a curious plight,
Missing in action, lost out of sight.
Clocks tick in circles, time does a dance,
Maybe it's magic, or just bad romance.

Lemons are yellow, but why not a blue?
The cats keep on plotting, they know more than you.
I tried to ask questions, but they just meowed,
Perhaps they're the wizards, with their heads proud.

Whispers of secrets in a bread box lie,
Who knew carbs could hold such a sly eye?
Pizza delivers answers, in cheesy delight,
But the toppings confuse; is it wrong or is right?

The world is my riddle, with laughter galore,
Every twist and turn opens hidden doors.
I'll crack all the codes, with a grin and a shout,
In this curious chase, what's life all about?

Reflections on a Murky Pond

A pond sits still, with secrets draped,
Frogs gossip softly, their tongues finely shaped.
I toss in a rock, the ripples do tease,
What's lurking beneath? A fish? Or a cheese?

The ducks quack in unison, a soundtrack of fun,
Do they ponder their future, or just bask in the sun?
I lean in close, the water's a friend,
But it's murky and muddy—will clarity end?

Reflections of clouds swirl askew in the haze,
Like jumbled up thoughts in a puzzling maze.
I'm searching for answers but all that I find,
Is the ripples of laughter that escape from my mind.

The reflections remind me, that life's quite the game,
With shadows and glitches, none of us the same.
In the murky depths, I chuckle with glee,
There's joy in the chaos, come splash here with me!

Puzzles in the Stars

Look up to the skies, decoding the night,
Stars twinkle and wink, oh what a sight!
Do they play hide and seek, so coy and aloof?
Or spin tales of mischief, far past our roof?

Constellations are stories, but what's the plot?
A bear meets a hunter? Or just random rot?
Galaxies giggle with cosmic delight,
As planets trip gracefully, through velvety night.

Astrologers ponder, with maps made of chalk,
While comets are cruising, they can't even walk.
Shooting stars pass; was that a wish or a fling?
The mysteries unfold in the push of a swing.

I gather my thoughts, and I ponder in spark,
The universe jokes in a beautiful arc.
Each riddle, each twinkle, each whirling surprise,
Is life just a game in the grandest of skies?

The Map of Introspection

I've charted my heart on a wrinkled old map,
X marks the spot, or perhaps it's a nap?
Every twist is a turn, every line is a clue,
Today I'll be wise, but tomorrow, who knew?

With crayons, I scribble my feelings and fears,
A treasure of giggles mixed into my tears.
The compass is broken; it spins round and round,
While my thoughts take a hike, where chaos is found.

I found an old sandwich from weeks past—oh dear,
Was it a relic, or just hunger's cruel sneer?
Maps don't show dinner, or paths to delight,
But I'll savor each moment, come day or come night.

Introspection's a riddle, with answers askew,
But I laugh at the journey, I waltz with my view.
Each detour and pitstop, a story to tell,
With each step I take, I'm investigatin' well!

The Threads that Bind

In a world of tangled strings,
I search for lost socks and things.
My cat leaps, oh what a sight,
Chasing dust motes in the light.

Grandma's wisdom, wrapped in yarn,
Knitting patterns, causing alarm.
"It's purling, dear, don't make a fuss!"
While I just sit, confused in the bus.

Friendships bloom like spider webs,
Sticky moments, that's how it ebbs.
Laughing at jokes that make no sense,
Life's a puzzle, let's commence!

So here's to threads that try to bind,
With goofy antics, you will find.
We're all stitches in the great big quilt,
Knotted together by the chaos built.

The Woven Stories of Us

With stories tangled, oh so bright,
We dance like shadows in the night.
A tale of tacos and lost keys,
My dog just snorts, he's quite at ease.

In coffee spills, our dreams collide,
Creating disasters we can't hide.
Together we laugh, creating noise,
Our lives a mix of silly joys.

Who stole the last piece of cake?
A mystery, for goodness' sake!
In laughter we find all the clues,
Like when I wore mismatched shoes.

So here we are, a woven bunch,
Delighting in every quirky hunch.
Through woven tales of twist and turn,
We celebrate what we can learn.

In Search of Missing Reflections

Looking for shoes that lost their mates,
In mirrors, I find new debates.
Is this me, reflected so fine?
Or is it just a trick of design?

The fridge hums a song of old,
While I ponder stories untold.
With my lunch, did I pack a grin?
Or simply forget where to begin?

Under the bed, monsters reside,
But I also found my old pride.
Searching for what I can't quite reach,
Every corner, a lesson to teach.

So grab a mirror, let's take a look,
At missing pieces of this goofy book.
I find reflections in every nook,
Even in chaos, I like how it shook.

Vignettes of the Undefined

In a world where truths twist and bend,
Each moment's a laugh, around the bend.
These vignettes dance like fireflies,
Lighting up our curious eyes.

The chocolate melts on a summer day,
While pigeons plot their next ballet.
With ice cream mustaches, we raise a cheer,
Creating memories, loud and clear.

What's next? A bubble or a prank?
As we plot mischief, with no rank.
A treasure map drawn in crayon hues,
Leading to adventure, with silly clues.

So here we gloat, undefined and free,
In a whimsical cage, just you and me.
Let's write our tales with a wink and a grin,
As the dance of unpredictability begins!

Essence of the Enigmatic

Why can't socks find their pair?
They vanish like dreams in thin air.
I search high and low, what a plight,
Just to wear shoes that feel right.

A cat sits judging my every move,
With a stare that's far from smooth.
Do they know more than they say?
Maybe I'm the fool in this fray.

The coffee spills, laughter ensues,
Another day of perplexing clues.
The whir of the blender, what a sound,
Was that a smoothie or lost intellect found?

With each tick of the clock, I blink,
Am I missing the point, or just on the brink?
Jigsaw pieces scatter, what do I glean?
Are we all part of some wild routine?

A Tangle of Hopes

I planted seeds of my grand design,
Watered them daily, told myself I'd shine.
Yet weeds grew up, what a surprise,
Not all sprouts are wise and wiseguys.

I sent my wishes to the stars,
But they returned like lost cars.
How can I steer my fate so fine,
When the GPS says 'car's out of line'?

Then there's the matter of my hair,
A tangle that screams 'beyond repair'.
I try to unravel knotted dreams,
But they laugh like mischievous schemes.

I dance like nobody's watching, it's true,
Yet the mirror shows a clown in a zoo.
As I tumble through life's playful jest,
Maybe being lost is just being blessed.

The Journey of Untold Stories

Each step I take, feels like a quest,
Chasing tales that never seem to rest.
I find a sock, a sandwich, a shoe,
But where's the adventure? I've barely a clue!

My shoes squeak louder than my thoughts,
In a world where reason often gets lost.
I scribble down notes on napkins and bags,
Hoping wisdom emerges from whimsical rags.

The bus driver sings off-key every day,
What a soundtrack for my rugged ballet!
I wave at pigeons, they strut like kings,
As the sun gives a wink before missing its fling.

With each misstep, a new plot twist,
It's hard to tell what I've truly missed.
Lessons disguised in laughter abound,
In this quirky tale, I'm happily drowned.

Finding Clarity in Chaos

In the kitchen chaos, I fish for a pan,
Only to stumble on burnt toast, oh man!
A recipe fails, what a hilarious scene,
I'm a master of mess, what does it mean?

My pet goldfish seems wise as a sage,
Staring at me like I'm stuck in a cage.
What wisdom does a bowl of water impart?
Perhaps simpler joys live in the heart.

With every dog bark and loose cat hair,
I laugh at the whirlwind swirling in air.
Clothes on the floor, where does it end?
Is the quest for order just around the bend?

Yet in this circus of quirky delight,
Every blunder brings smiles, so bright.
A dance in the chaos, a jig in disguise,
Maybe the fun is just seeing through wise.

The Art of Questioning

Why does the sun rise and fall,
Is it tired, or having a ball?
Do fish think they're on a trip?
Or just swimming with no end in grip?

What's the deal with socks and shoes?
Do they argue, or just snooze?
Is cheese a friend or foe?
I hope it doesn't spoil my flow!

Why do spoons prefer the soup?
And forks become part of the group?
Are ants having a tiny parade?
Or is it just a kitchen charade?

Can a cat ever truly know
Why humans chase them to and fro?
Is every meow a question too?
In this circus, what's real and what's true?

The Search for Missing Pieces

Where did that sock go again?
Did it flee to a sock-filled den?
Why do puzzle pieces play tricks?
Hiding from me, those sneaky bricks!

Is a cookie really just a cake?
Or a riddle waiting to break?
Do shadows have a life of their own?
Or are they just perils that've grown?

What if the minute hand does sprint?
And hours just think they're a hint?
Can a lost key really roam free?
Or is it hiding under the sea?

I swear I had a plan today,
But plans seem to wiggle away!
As if the universe has a laugh,
While I'm busy chasing my other half!

Chasing Shadows of Truth

Why do shadows seem so sly?
Are they just light's little lie?
Do they whisper secrets at night?
Or only dance till the morning light?

What if rainbows are just beams?
With colors borrowed from our dreams?
Is the sun playing peek-a-boo?
While the clouds giggle, it's true?

Do mirrors hold a cheeky sway?
Reflecting half the words we say?
Is laughter a sound or a game?
That wraps us up in fun and fame?

Why does the moon look down and grin?
As if keeping secrets wrapped within?
Is every star a twinkle in jest?
Whispering tales they wish to test?

The Tapestry of Experience

What flavors does wisdom taste?
Is it sweet, or just a waste?
Are memories like threads that weave?
Or just swaps we can't retrieve?

Is laughter the glue that holds us tight?
Or just a spark that takes flight?
Do friendships come with user guides?
Or are they just wild, carefree rides?

If mischief is the spice of life,
Can boredom be a cutting knife?
Are hiccups just life's funny dance?
Or a challenge to take a chance?

Can we blend our tales with a cheer?
As we navigate this puzzling sphere?
Is every stumble part of the race?
Or a giggle in this grand embrace?

Pieces of a Hidden Puzzle

I found a piece under my bed,
It must have come from my old shed.
The cat sits there, a watchful spy,
While I ponder why I can't fly.

My socks betrayed me, scattered wide,
Like clues that vanish, I can't abide.
A puzzle box needs just one swap,
But I've misplaced the piece on top.

With every giggle from the floor,
The colors swirl, a vibrant score.
A wrong turn leads to a surprising feat,
I laugh at all the missing meat.

In this game where I take my time,
Each step I take feels like a rhyme.
A chuckle here, a wink from fate,
And I smile at the twist of fate.

The Enigma of Everyday Moments

A coffee cup, half full with foam,
With sprinkles that remind me of home.
The toast pops up, a golden treat,
I'll take the crumbs, can't taste defeat.

Traffic jams bring laughter's roar,
As I count the cows that cross the floor.
Each honk a song that joins the dance,
In this odd waltz, I take a chance.

I squabble with the mailman's hat,
While dodging squirrels upon a mat.
Every door I open creaks and groans,
Yet somehow feels like my very own.

When the sun dips low, I run and slide,
Through puddles formed from life's sweet ride.
With every step, the laughter grows,
In moments missed, the fun still flows.

Shadows in the Sunlight

When I walk, my shadow plays,
A silly dance that always sways.
It ducks and dives behind my knee,
Chasing after what it can't see.

The grass tickles my toes all day,
While clouds debate if they should stay.
My hat flies off in playful glee,
I chase it down, oh what a spree!

Laughter hides behind garden walls,
Where dandelions play in stalls.
The sun winks down, a cheeky tease,
As I twirl 'round like a summer breeze.

With each bright beam that lights the ground,
A silly song is all around.
This dance with shadows brings delight,
Life's quirkiness, a true sunlight.

Secrets Beneath the Surface

There's a goldfish spinning tales,
With secrets swaying in its scales.
It whispers things to my pet cat,
Who plots escape and can't sit flat.

Underwater bubbles rise anew,
Each one a hope, a laugh or two.
In every ripple, truth might hide,
As laughter echoes, side by side.

Under the rocks, the mysteries creep,
As I tiptoe like a spy, not deep.
What on earth could the fish expose?
Maybe the secret of garden gnomes!

So I keep searching, eyeing each wave,
Finding joy in what makes me brave.
Beneath the surface, a jolly whirl,
A chuckle shared with every twirl.

Dancing with the Unknown

In socks that slide across the floor,
I twirl with fate, then ask for more.
The music plays, a quirky tune,
I dance with shadows beneath the moon.

The fridge hums loud, a partner near,
It whispers things I cannot hear.
With each misstep, I giggle bright,
The unknown steps on my feet tonight.

Around the corner, a cat appears,
Chasing my thoughts, mocking my fears.
I leap and laugh, we weave and spin,
In this grand waltz, where do I begin?

Oh, let the stars guide my next move,
For in this dance, I surely groove.
With every laugh, a question plops,
What happens next? The music stops!

The Murmur of Unanswered Questions

I woke up puzzled, had a dream,
Where squirrels led a secret team.
They plotted schemes, all kinds of fun,
To steal my snacks and run, run, run!

Over coffee, I pondered in glee,
Why can't I speak fluent bee?
I'd ask them all about the hive,
And join their buzz, feel so alive!

But time's a thief, it steals away,
As I sip my brew and start to sway.
With questions swirling like cream in cup,
I try to solve, but where's my luck?

Are ducks just chickens in disguise?
I laugh and sigh as time just flies.
Unraveling threads that life spun tight,
With unanswered truths, I sleep tonight.

Whispers of the Unseen

The toaster popped, it sang, it laughed,
A breakfast dance, oh what a craft!
Yet as I buttered my golden slice,
The toaster winked; was that too nice?

Invisible beings, oh so sly,
Haunting my cereal, oh my my!
Is that a ghost with a sugary cheer?
I'd ask them for tips, but they disappear!

On the bus, a seat for one,
Bumps and jostles, oh the fun!
Does this driver know where we go?
With wrong turns taken, we steal the show!

As sirens wail and streetlights blink,
I laugh at the chaos, don't want to think.
The day unfolds with questions galore,
What are we here for? And so much more!

Threads of the Unknown

In my closet, I found a sock,
It whispered secrets, tickled my clock.
Missing its mate, a tale to tell,
Of laundry rooms and soap, oh well!

The cat stares hard; it knows too much,
Plotting his schemes with a knowing touch.
Is he the mastermind of my day?
Or just a fluffball in disarray?

Balloons in the sky, they float and tease,
What dreams do they hold with such sweet ease?
I wave them a goodbye, with hope so bright,
They take my worries far outta sight.

Each thread tangled, I'll unravel still,
With laughter and joy, it's quite the thrill.
The questions line up like a train on tracks,
And I'll ride this journey, no looking back!

Steps Through a Veiled Journey

I tripped on a shoelace today,
Fell right into a pile of hay.
Thought I saw the truth in that mess,
But hey, at least I had a good guess.

With a compass that spins like a cat,
And a map drawn by my hungry brat.
I'm dancing on paths both twisted and bent,
Trying to find where my days went.

The signs all point in every direction,
I'm lost in a maze of pure reflection.
But laughter echoes through every hall,
Even when I'm stumbling, I stand tall.

So here's to the quests that make us grin,
And the surprises tucked under our skin.
For every riddle I fail to untie,
There's a chuckle waiting, oh my oh my!

Moments of Disquiet

Why do socks always go astray?
One missing, the other in dismay.
I search the world, a wild sock thief,
While laughter chases away my grief.

A cat that knows too much for sure,
Looks me in the eye with a purr.
Do they hold the answers to my plight?
Or just enjoy my silly fright?

I ponder in circles like a rolling stone,
While my plants whisper secrets, all alone.
They thrive in the chaos of my messy room,
Confident in their leafy bloom.

And so I giggle at the thoughts that weigh,
Finding delight in the foolish fray.
For in the oddities, I find my cheer,
With every moment, I hold dear.

Searching for the Key

I lost my keys beneath a chair,
A scavenger hunt, it's only fair.
Searching under the couch with a sigh,
Should have planted a GPS sky high.

The fridge hums secrets, cold and deep,
While I ponder where my patience keeps.
Each drawer a riddle, each shelf a tease,
But laughter keeps me afloat with ease.

My dog watches, eyes full of glee,
As I dance for my missing safety key.
He thinks it's a game, and in his bark,
I find the light in the hidden dark.

With every clatter of pots and pans,
I embrace the chaos, make my plans.
For every key that's ever slipped away,
There's a chuckle waiting at the end of the day.

Beyond the Veil of Certainty

Peeking through curtains, what do I see?
A world of wonders puzzling me.
Answers flutter like moths in the light,
I chase them down, what a silly sight!

The clouds debate on what's next to come,
While ants march in lines, a tiny drum.
I'm left here wondering what all this means,
As I sip my tea, plotting my schemes.

The toaster burns bread, starts a small fire,
And the cat's on the roof, climbing higher.
Do they know more than I ever will?
My mystery friends give me quite the thrill.

So I'll laugh at the riddles life throws my way,
And gather my thoughts during each crazy day.
For behind every veil lies a wacky delight,
Just waiting for someone to join the flight!

A Tidal Wave of Questions

Why do socks disappear in the wash?
They're plotting a getaway, oh what a nosh!
What's the secret of the universe?
Is it found in a dog's latest verse?

Why do chairs insist on being so tall?
Yet, the table seems to have no care at all!
Will I ever make sense of the things I eat?
Especially that mysterious gummy treat?

Clarity in the Clouds

Clouds puffy like marshmallows in the sky,
Do they ever wonder why they float so high?
When I try to count them, they just blend,
Is that their way of teasing me, my friend?

Is the sun's smile a reflection of cheer?
Or does it just giggle at me down here?
With sunsets painting colors so bright,
Are rainbows just the weather's delight?

Dreaming in the Twilight

As twilight tucks in the day with a sigh,
Do fireflies hold secret parties nearby?
Can dreams tell me what socks I should choose?
Or just play tricks, leaving me confused?

If I chase a shadow, where would it go?
Should I ask the cats who seem to know?
Whispers in the twilight, full of cheer,
Is it snack time yet, or is that just me here?

The Road Under Stars

Stars twinkle like they're lost in a dance,
Are they critiquing my poor moonlit prance?
On this road, with crickets serenading me,
Are the bumps just jokes from the universe, you see?

Do constellations scribble stories above?
Or are they merely a shimmering love?
Do the owls discuss their nocturnal spree,
While I try hard not to trip on a tree?

The Labyrinth Within

In the maze of my mind, I dance with glee,
Finding my socks, and where could they be?
Chasing my thoughts, like cats on a spree,
Mapping out secrets, like treasure to see.

I ask myself questions, both silly and grand,
Why did I walk in here without a plan?
With snacks as my guide, I gallivant and stand,
In circles I wander, just holding my hand.

The walls of confusion, they laugh in delight,
As I trip on my shoelaces, lost in the night.
With humor as fuel, I continue the fight,
Unlocking my riddles while eating a bite.

So here in this labyrinth, I'll twirl and I'll spin,
Embracing the chaos, with laughter akin.
For every dead end, there's always a grin,
In the maze of my mind, the fun will begin.

Every Breath a Riddle

The morning yawns wide, it tickles my nose,
Why do we dream about wearing strange clothes?
With coffee in hand, I ponder and pose,
Each breath is a riddle, and who really knows?

I met a wise bird with a curious tune,
He told me to dance when the light turned to moon.
With giggles and wiggles, I hum along soon,
Breathing in questions, floating like a balloon.

The tickles of laughter, they bubble and burst,
What if the answers are quenchless, like thirst?
With a wink and a nod, I ride the mad burst,
Seeking the strange in the normal, immersed.

So I laugh with my breath, a riddle's embrace,
Finding joy in the chaos, a whimsical race.
With each silly moment, I wear a big face,
The riddle of breathing is my favorite chase.

Unfolding the Spiral

In a world of spirals, I twirl with delight,
Chasing my shadows, oh what a sight!
Each spin is a giggle, as day turns to night,
Untangling the twist, I hold on so tight.

A chicken crossed roads, but I lost track of time,
Did I miss the punchline or just rhyme for a dime?
With a fork and a spoon, I'm searching for prime,
In the spiral of life, it's all about mime.

What's left in the cupboard? More questions to laze,
As I float through the swirl, caught up in the maze.
With pasta for wisdom, my mind goes ablaze,
Unfolding the spiral, I dance in a daze.

So here's to the journey, the spin and the whirl,
In the spiral of wonders, I oddly unfurl.
With laughter as music, I frolic and twirl,
In absurdity's arms, around I will swirl.

The Puzzle I Carry

With pieces scattered, I gather my thoughts,
Got a puzzle of wisdom, tied up in knots.
Is there a corner where logic forgot?
Or did I lose patience inside all the spots?

Each piece holds a chuckle, a giggle or sigh,
Finding the edges, the cat watches nearby.
"Where does this piece go?" I ask in a cry,
But he just rolls over and blinks with an eye.

I fumble and fidget, my brain feels so free,
Trying my best to fit pieces with glee.
With pink and with purple, the colors agree,
That life's just a puzzle, but funny as can be.

So I savor the process, each piece I embrace,
In the funny little gaps, I'll find my own space.
For the puzzle I carry will always leave trace,
That laughter and chaos are part of the race.

Chasing Fleeting Dreams

I chased a cloud that looked like cheese,
But it rained instead, oh how to appease!
A squirrel stole my sandwich, quick as a flash,
While I stood perplexed, observing the clash.

With every step, I trip over fate,
Falling headfirst into a plate of cake.
I dance with shadows that mock my strides,
As I ponder where this silliness hides.

The mirror laughs back; it's hard to pretend,
That youth didn't fade like the grass in the end.
Chasing dreams feels like running through sand,
What's just out of reach? Now, that's unplanned!

Yet I skip along this ludicrous track,
With giggles that echo and no turning back.
Perhaps the punchline lies down the road,
In the riddle of living, it's quite the load!

The Tapestry of Tomorrow

I wove a dream from spaghetti strands,
Measured by laughter, not by demands.
With sauce for joy and a side of cheer,
Tomorrow's tapestry is knitted right here.

Pinches of hope, and a sprinkle of fate,
Is this too much? Or am I just great?
A dog wearing glasses sits on my lap,
Guarding the secret of this funny-map.

The future's a jigsaw of mismatched pieces,
Where wisdom and giggles are what never ceases.
I thread the needle with a grin quite wide,
Stitching each moment where giggles reside.

In patterns of chaos, I thrive and spin,
Finding the joy in where troubles begin.
Threads of the past may tangle and twine,
Yet, the quirky tapestry always will shine!

Dreams Beneath the Surface

Beneath the waves of a waffle cone,
Lie dreams of sprinkles; I'm never alone.
Swirling in syrup and filled with delight,
My ambition floats past a jellyfish bite.

I dug for treasure in my cereal bowl,
And found a prize that made breakfast whole.
A marshmallow island, with gumdrop shores,
Who knew this chaos could open such doors?

Splashing through puddles of fizzy soda,
I ask the goldfish if they know the quota.
"Can I trade a wish for a daring leap?"
They blink in response, now I can't sleep!

So here's to the dreams that bubble and rise,
Wrapped in the giggles as laughter complies.
Delving deep down, this riddle's absurd,
I'll crack root beer floats for each solemn word!

Between the Lines of Existence

Between the lines, I doodle my fate,
In margins of notebooks, I contemplate.
A tango with pencils, a waltz with the eraser,
Each doodle reveals a quirky chaser.

Tickling the edges of reasonable thought,
I scribble in colors that can't be bought.
An avocado wearing a tiny crown,
Is this the wisdom that will not drown?

With every question, I draw a mustache,
Swaying to laughter, not needing to dash.
Coffee spills secrets from the brink of a cup,
In this whimsical tale, I feel the hiccup!

Existence is wrapped in a riddle-like game,
Where puns take flight and the humor's aflame.
In doodles and sketches, the answers may hide,
While fun dances free like a wobbly tide!

Echoes of an Untold Journey

I packed my bags for a trip,
Yet forgot where I was going.
Google Maps said turn left,
But my heart was still snowing.

The train was late, oh so late,
I laughed and missed my stop.
With snacks in tow, I felt great,
Guess I'll just roam till I drop.

I met a cat who wore a tie,
Said he'd run for mayor one day.
I asked him how, he winked an eye,
"Just purr-suade them," he'd say.

Each twist and turn, a curious plight,
With riddles tossed, I danced along.
In echoes of laughter, all feels right,
This journey's tune, a joyous song.

The Riddle of the Rising Sun

The morning light peeks through the blinds,
Who turned on the bright, shiny glare?
I squint and search for lost designs,
In hair that looks like a bear.

My coffee's cold, a bitter tease,
I spill it down my favorite shirt.
Now I'm dressed for a caffeine breeze,
Fashion's lost, but hey, it's dessert!

The sun and I play hide and seek,
It giggles as it rises high.
With shadows stretching, feeling chic,
I trip, but still, I'll touch the sky.

Each dawn unfolds like a wild riddle,
I laugh and tumble on the fun.
With every giggle and little twiddle,
The day once more has just begun.

Footprints in the Fog

I wandered out into the mist,
My shoes squelched on a soggy floor.
Lost in dreams and a drowsy twist,
I waved at a ghost, or maybe more.

Each step I took, a woeful chance,
Do I glide or merely stumble?
A dance of fate, a silly prance,
Then face-first in the fog, I tumbled.

A squirrel laughed and shared its nuts,
"I wouldn't do that if I were you."
But I was trying to avoid the ruts,
Now I'm just one with the dew.

The fog may hide those paths ahead,
But giggles rise like morning light.
With each odd turn, by humor led,
I'll surf this haze till the night.

Unfolding the Veil

I peeked behind a curtain's fold,
To find a world of quirky beasts.
There's dancing frogs and cakes of gold,
And a parrot who tells jokes at feasts.

"Why did the banana cross the street?"
The parrot squawked, all eyes turned wide.
"To peel out fast and skip a beat!"
Laughter echoed, no reason to hide.

In dreams where silliness reigns supreme,
I strolled through a land made of pie.
Unwrapping hope like some grand scheme,
With sprinkles above and jam in the sky.

So here's to the wonders we pursue,
With giggles wrapped in laughter's sail.
Each layer peeled reveals the new,
In this wild dance of the veil.

The Unsung Narratives

In the giggles of dawn, where shadows play,
I tripped on my shoelace and fell in a sway.
The cat gave a wink, with a tail so grand,
As if to declare, "You don't understand!"

A squirrel in a suit tried to offer me cheese,
While jumping on branches with utmost ease.
I pondered his wisdom in a nutty tone,
Thinking perhaps, I should follow his own!

A clock on the wall chimed just to confuse,
Saying it's dinner when it's really shoes.
The dog rolled his eyes at my hungry plight,
As I melted my soup with a fork - what a sight!

So here in this tale with its quirks and spins,
I scribble my notes on what makes us grin.
Each twist brings a laugh, each turn brings a cheer,
In this lively adventure, I've nothing to fear!

Signposts in the Dark

Stumbling through shadows, I chase after dreams,
Finding a sandwich, or so it seems.
The light above flickers, a disco ball dance,
While I pet a lamp that thought it could prance.

My map is a puzzle with pieces all tossed,
And the directions I'm given just leave me lost.
Yet a signpost appears that says 'Go to the fun!'
I follow its lead, and then I just run!

There's laughter around me in every odd place,
A zebra on roller skates, what a wild race!
The grass is all blue, and the clouds wear a grin,
As I juggle my worries, and let the joy in.

Through mazes of chuckles, I wander and sway,
Unraveling moments in a silly ballet.
With every misstep, I dance my own spark,
In the quirkiest places, I find my own mark!

The Canvas of Conundrums

Splashing in colors, my brush makes a mess,
As I paint some confusion, I must confess.
With squirrels as models and cupcakes for round,
I giggle at all the strange things that I've found.

A puzzle of turtles in fuzzy blue hats,
Join choir with ducks, on the backs of their mats.
Each stroke tells a story that's silly and bright,
In a world full of giggles that dance in the light.

But what is the meaning of purple and gold?
Why do the worm and the cactus feel bold?
I ponder these questions as laughter erupts,
In this canvas of chaos, where conundrums are cupped!

So hand me my brush, let's create with delight,
A masterpiece full of mischief and light.
As the world swirls around with its magical spin,
I'll color outside lines, where the fun will begin!

Tangles of Wonder

In the web of my thoughts, I'm lost in a haze,
Twisted and tangled in humorous ways.
A shoelace, a spider, a sock with a hole,
And laughter erupts as I ponder my role.

The mirror is laughing, a trickster's delight,
With a face that is squishy from last night's bite.
A rabbit appears, wearing glasses so big,
Asking me questions, while doing a jig.

A blender debates if it's soup or a shake,
Sipping on flavors that wobble and quake.
While the toaster speaks wisdom from crumbs left behind,

As I jot down the nonsense, quite crazy and kind.

So here I am, swirling in laughter and fun,
On this pathway of puzzles, where nonsense is spun.
Each tangle a story, a giggle, a thrill,
In the circus of wonder, I'm dancing at will!

The Inkwell of Possibilities

In a world of inkblots, I scribble away,
With quill in one hand, I dance and I play.
Chasing my thoughts like a cat on the run,
Each page is a puzzle, each riddle, a pun.

I trip on the phrases that jump off the page,
Finding new stories that fit like a cage.
I mix up my colors, I blend shades of joy,
In this comedy sketch, I'm my own favorite toy.

With questions that jiggle and twirl in my mind,
I chase after answers, elusive, unkind.
The more that I write, the less that I see,
It's just me and my inkwell, as lively as can be.

Every drop holds a secret, a thought or a laugh,
I'm lost in this journey, with no need for a map.
So here's to the chaos, the giggles, the cheer,
In the world of possibilities, boredom's not near.

Uncharted Waters of Being

I sail on a boat made of giggles and dreams,
With oars made of laughter and a sail that beams.
Each wave carries questions that splash with great force,
While I navigate waters without any course.

A mermaid waves hello, with a wink and a flip,
She hands me a treasure map, says, 'Take a trip!'
I dive in the deep where the weird fish swim by,
Chasing clues to the meaning, or at least, the pie.

The seagulls squawk riddles that tickle my ears,
As I float through the moments, both joyful and weird.
The tides twist and turn like a dance on the shore,
In uncharted waters, who could ask for more?

With each splash that I make, I giggle and grin,
In a sea of confusion, I plot my next win.
So let's toast with coconut drinks on the beach,
For the thrill of the search is the dream that we reach.

The Search for Meaning

With a magnifying glass, I scan every nook,
Trying to find answers in every good book.
The wise owls just hoot, and the rabbits just laugh,
As I ponder and puzzle through each little gaffe.

I ask the clouds questions; they shuffle and sigh,
'We're busy floating by; that's our alibi.'
And the moon winks down, full of secrets and charms,
While I chase cosmic lessons, escaping their arms.

The signs on the streets seem to giggle and tease,
With arrows that point in all directions, but please!
The treasure I seek is not gold or a ring,
But a chuckle, a smile, the joy that they bring.

I pen down my findings in messy old prose,
With laughter and wisdom, who truly knows?
So I continue my quest, with a twinkle in eye,
For the punchlines of wisdom are worth every try.

Flickers of the Profound

In the mundane hustle, I pause and I stare,
At a flicker of wisdom dancing through the air.
Like fireflies buzzing in the warm summer night,
They blink with a message, a wink of delight.

I survey the horizon with a grin on my face,
For chaos and humor bring joy to the chase.
In a world full of quirks, let confusion be king,
As I juggle the questions like a clown with a swing.

Moments hit hard, like a pie in the sky,
Your answer is waiting; just give it a try.
The profound can be silly, wrapped up in a smile,
So I dance with confusion, it's worth every mile.

With snickers and chuckles, I ride the great wave,
Through the absurdities, I am, oh so brave.
So let's raise a toast to the flickers, the jest,
In this grand comedy, it's humor that's best.

The Quest for Clarity

In the morning, I search for my keys,
Only to find them stuck in my sleeve.
The cat stares, judging my plight,
As I wonder, is this wrong or right?

The coffee spills, I laugh at the mess,
I think, maybe I'm just too blessed.
My socks still mismatched, oh what a scene,
In a world where normal's just a mean.

My plans go awry, like a kite in a tree,
I chase after hopes, but they flutter from me.
With every mistake, I learn to embrace,
The thrill of the stumble, the joy of the chase.

So here I stand, in my quirky parade,
With laughter in hand and worries delayed.
For answers aren't found in a straight, tidy line,
But in twists, turns, and a glass of good wine.

Dance of the Unfathomable

I stepped on my shoe, and the dog gave a bark,
As I tripped over dreams that sailed in the dark.
The universe grins at my clumsy charade,
While I chuckle, not fearing my messy crusade.

Is that cheese on my shirt? Or a new fashion trend?
My mirror reflects a delightful pretend.
I twirl through the chaos, missing the beat,
But my heart feels the rhythm; oh, it's quite the feat!

In this dance of unknowns, I step on some toes,
With giggles erupting from laughter that grows.
The unexpected spins lead me off course,
Yet somehow I feel I'm a part of the force.

So bring on the shuffle, the jig and the jive,
With mishaps and laughter, I'm glad I'm alive.
For without all the stumbles, where would I be?
Just a shadow of normal, not truly me.

Echoes of Questions Untold

What's for dinner? Is it Tuesday or Friday?
My calendar laughs, like, 'Good luck, my friend!'
The clock ticks away, and I ponder my fate,
As I rummage for snacks—my ultimate state!

Did I water that plant? Did I feed the void?
I shout to the heavens for the answers deployed.
The universe giggles, resounding its cheer,
While I blink at the lightbulb, just waiting to clear.

Questions abound like leaves in the breeze,
Why do I trip on imaginary knees?
I scribble in circles, the page full of doubts,
Yet each laugh and each grin give my heart a good shout.

So I'll soak in confusion and dance with a smile,
Embracing the chaos; no need for denial.
For echoes of questions, they freely unfold,
Creating my story, both funny and bold.

The River of Unanswered Thoughts

Down by the river, my thoughts take a swim,
They dive and they splash, each one looking grim.
What's the meaning of socks? Or pancakes at dawn?
I chase after the answers, but they play and they fawn.

The sun shines brightly, the fish giggle loud,
While I ponder my purpose amidst the crowd.
I toss in my worries, watch them float away,
They wave back to me, saying, 'We're here to play!'

With each wave of the water, a silly new tale,
Of ducks in top hats riding a snail.
So I whisper to them, "Oh, give me a sign!"
But they wave with abandon, sipping on brine.

So here in this river, where thoughts swirl like tea,
I'll gather the silly, let my spirit run free.
For the answers may linger, like stars up above,
Yet it's laughter and wonder that fill me with love.

Resilient in the Unknown

Woke up today, shoes on the wrong feet,
Coffee's a puzzle I can't quite defeat.
Chasing my cat, we both take a slide,
Turns out he's the wise one, oh what a ride!

Lost my keys in the fridge, who put them there?
Searching for answers in the middle of air.
Dance with the socks that are stubbornly lost,
In this baffling waltz, it's all about the cost.

Every mishap a riddle, a joke on my brain,
Laughter erupts like a runaway train.
With each little trip, I just roll on the floor,
A master of chaos, who could ask for more?

So here's to the blunders that make my day bright,
In the land of confusion, I'm full of delight.
Embracing the quirks in this playful charade,
Each twist and each turn, a grand escapade!

The Unfurling Scroll

Waking each day like a scroll with no end,
Untangling stories, around every bend.
Breakfast confetti, there's cereal on the wall,
Each splatter a feature in this banquet hall!

The toaster just smirked as the bagel took flight,
Pop! went the drama, oh what a sight!
Unfolding my plans with a whimsical flair,
Next stop is the fridge—what's the mystery there?

A sock in the toaster, a joke I can tell,
Navigating nonsense, I'm under a spell.
Each twist on my path is a giggle or two,
Like knitting with pasta, what's my next cue?

So here's to the scroll that keeps rolling, it seems,
Whispers of laughter and nibbled-up dreams.
In a world full of burbles and hiccups galore,
I pen down the chaos and always want more!

A Symphony of Unspoken Thoughts

Woke up with music ringing in my head,
A symphony of chaos where sanity fled.
The cereal's crunching a wild cacophony,
My blender's a soloist, filled with irony!

Each thought is a note in a jazz jam I make,
Prancing in pajamas, oh, for heaven's sake!
Every quiet moment's an unexpected show,
Singing with socks as I dance to and fro.

The clock's ticking loudly, a drum with no beat,
In this fun little concert, I can't find my seat.
With giggles and glimmers, I twirl 'round the room,
My house just a stage for the quirks to consume!

So here's to the laughter and music so bright,
Each crescendo of silliness shining with light.
In the concert of nonsense, I'll take my sweet stand,
A maestro of mayhem, with chaos unplanned!

The Shadow of What Could Be

In the corner, a shadow is plotting away,
What if it dances on a sunbeam today?
It whispers of mischief, it giggles and grins,
Like socks in a dryer, it spins and it spins.

Today I might tumble, trip, or just flop,
But watch out, dear shadow, I'm ready to hop!
Each stumble's a riddle, each fall's a delight,
It beckons me forward with mischievous fright.

What could be hiding behind every door?
A treasure of giggles, or maybe some more?
I'll chase down the shadows, let them guide me through,
To the whimsy and wonders, both old and brand new!

So come take this journey, let's see where we go,
With humor and laughter, let imagination flow.
In the dance of the shadows, there's magic I see,
And the joy of discovery, oh, it's wild and free!

www.ingramcontent.com/pod-product-compliance
Lightning Source LLC
Chambersburg PA
CBHW072132070526
44585CB00016B/1645